One of the many guide stoops (pillars) on the moors above Sheffield, near Bradfield. R may indicate 'royal', possibly a local form of 'customary' mile. Similar stones are found in Derbyshire, on the moors, for example above Holymoorside.

Milestones

Mervyn Benford

Published by Shire Publications Ltd,
Midland House, West Way, Botley, Oxford OX2 0PH.
(Website: www.shirebooks.co.uk)

Copyright © 2002 by Mervyn Benford.
First published 2002.
Transferred to digital print on demand 2011.
Shire Library 401. ISBN 978 0 74780 526 7.
Mervyn Benford is hereby identified as the author of this
work in accordance with Section 77 of the Copyright,
Designs and Patents Act 1988.

British Library Cataloguing in Publication Data:
Benford, Mervyn
Milestones. – (A Shire book; 401)
1. Milestones – Great Britain – History
I. Title
388.1'3'0941'09
ISBN-10 0 7478 0526 1
ISBN-13 978 0 74780 526 7

This book is dedicated to the memory of Ken Diamond, who for more than fifty years
photographed over two thousand milestones. The Ken Diamond archive has been lodged with
the Milestone Society. Many thanks are also owed to Val for her patience, enthusiasm and
encouragement.

Cover: *Left: An example showing miles, furlongs and poles from the A380 Exeter-Torquay road, now a dual carriageway, just south of Kennford; Devon has several examples using these old measures. Top right: A Welsh example close to Lampeter. This is the only known milestone left with reference to the original method of measurement, namely sightmen, who are named as Timothy Jacob and Samuel Davies, and who worked by line of sight. Bottom Right: A fine example of several very detailed markers in Fife, listing many very small places; this one is on the B9171 near Killie Castle in the Largo area.*

Printed in Great Britain by PrintOnDemand-Worldwide.com, Peterborough, UK.

Contents

A restored plate on an old Gloucestershire mounting block on the B4070 near Painswick, which used to be the main road between Cheltenham and Stroud.

The origin of milestones

Although significant routes across England already existed in the Iron Age the Romans, who first came to Britain in 55 BC and later settled in AD 43, needed a better network of roads. Julius Caesar himself probably used those original prehistoric track routes, such as the Icknield Way. To move soldiers and supplies fast, the Romans laid good, metalled roads, many echoed in major routes today. Others show on maps as straight stretches of minor roads or tracks. The Romans measured distance to aid timing and efficiency, marking every thousandth double-step pace with a large circular stone (Latin *mille* = 'thousand'). The distance so measured was 1618 yards, close to the eventual British standard mile of 1760 yards.

Some stones were uninscribed; others gave route distances and occasionally a dedication, which helps date them. Not surprisingly, given the relatively less developed societies that ensued, very few remain *in situ*. However, on the road to Vindolanda fort, close to Hadrian's Wall, one plain stone remains where it has stood for two thousand years, with another, broken one a Roman mile westward. Near Sedbergh in Cumbria another stone is believed locally to be Roman. A Latin text carved in 1836 records a contemporary effort at

A Roman milestone in situ at Vindolanda near Hadrian's Wall.

This stone near Cowan Bridge in Lancashire on the line of the old Roman road from Ribchester is possibly Roman but it has modern information.

recognition and conservation. Others survive in museums close to former major Roman centres.

From time to time stones are found which may be Roman. One hides in vegetation near an old Severn crossing in Gloucestershire. Records note that four stones once stood on this route but none is supposed to be Roman. Another that hints of Roman origins stands equally shy where the trackway across the Bowland Fells from Ribchester in Lancashire joins a country road into Cowan Bridge on the A65. Careful examination reveals later inscriptions giving directions to two local hamlets but these could have been carved on a pre-existing stone.

The records of museums, libraries and universities, and of organisations serving walkers and cyclists, can reveal early references to milestones, guideposts, roads, routes and travel. Cyclists and walkers may

New Forest ponies and a milestone near Burley, Hampshire.

Two well-maintained metal mile-markers, from Leicestershire (left) and Warwickshire (right), photographed for their aesthetic appeal.

often use old, redundant roads that are now just tracks and paths. In 1936 S. E. Winbolt used old records to calculate the precise location of sixty-one milestones flanking the Roman Stane Street through Sussex. Milestones turn up in some very attractive settings. From about 1880 cyclists organised races with milestones defining the start, finish and turning points.

John Ogilby and the development of roads in the seventeenth century

After the Romans left Britain in the fifth century their roads progressively declined. The feudal system tied most people to their home villages. Tax collectors, troops and aristocratic families might undertake lengthy journeys but they were always dangerous. Saxon and medieval societies had a less developed idea of national communication, using local routes that were little better than uneven, narrow and often muddy tracks.

As trade and urban life developed, something akin to a national network gradually evolved. In 1660 the General Letter Office was established but few roads were suited to conveying mail by post-coach. Moreover, the varying lengths of 'customary' miles inhibited a fair charging system. At the end of the seventeenth century, during the reign of William and Mary, a hundred years after the introduction of the 1760 yard statute mile in 1593, people were still complaining of the 'long' miles found in Yorkshire and other places, over 2600 yards in some areas. The mail system, with the charge based on the distance travelled, needed standard miles.

The quality and extent of the road network interested Charles II and encouraged him to support a proposal by John Ogilby (1600–76) to survey the nation's roads. Ogilby began his survey in the early 1670s, the first cartographer to use the 'new' statute mile. He dedicated his atlas of a hundred fine and accurate maps published in 1675, with three further editions the same year, to the King and earned the splendid title of 'Cosmographer to His Majestie'. This alone encouraged the support of others and helped considerably when he faced local opposition in conducting his survey.

At the end of the seventeenth century existing county maps by cartographers like Saxton only inadequately represented roads. Ogilby's small team of surveyors literally walked the nation's roads, measuring distances, angular directions and road inclines. They used a wheel dimensurator, a device finely engineered to record 10 statute miles in just one revolution. The nature of the exercise is well encapsulated in one of the cartouches decorating four of the maps.

Ogilby's team marked each mile on strips, his very original device to cover up to 70 linear miles on one map page (modern road atlases record motorways similarly). Marking the miles did not imply the existence of milestones, but one two-mile stone is noted and there are references to mile-markers near racecourses. Ogilby had funds for no more than a hundred major routes (although he surveyed many more) and this may explain why some towns such as Liverpool do not feature in his atlas. Many of the routes recorded by

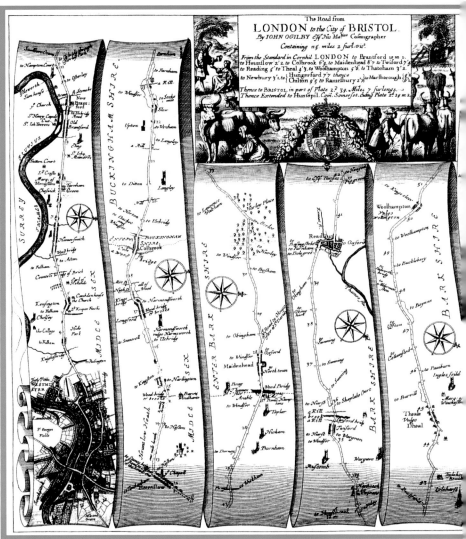

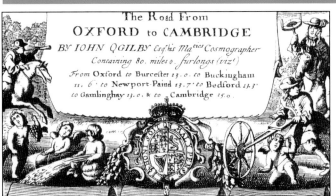

A map (above) and cartouche (left) from John Ogilby's road atlas of 1675.

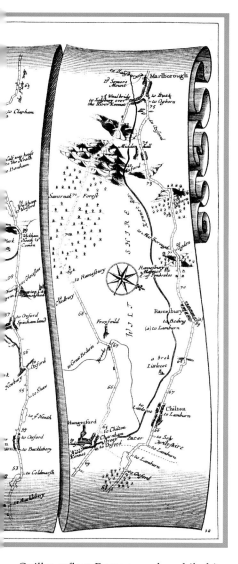

Ogilby reflect Roman roads, while his maps defined travel for the next three centuries. Although as a dancing master he had earlier been Master of the King's Revels in Ireland, Ogilby did not cover Ireland in his survey. The road to Holyhead, however, was the principal route to Ireland for government officials, and Telford set stones on the Irish side in exactly the same style when he renewed the entire London to Holyhead road.

The maps are a useful introduction to the nature of travel at the time. They laid the ground for the universal use of the statute mile, a standard eventually etched indelibly into the national consciousness by milestones.

9

The Pen-y-bryn tollbridge joins the A493 and A496 roads across the head of the Barmouth estuary near Dolgellau in Gwynedd.

Turnpike trusts and milestones

Developing postal services brought increased travel by road. Mail-coaches ran regularly to schedules and passengers travelled widely. The new excitement of travel encouraged various individuals and local communities to erect obelisks and other pillars inscribed with guidance for travellers. The earliest known instance of a road being marked in miles was that from Dover to Canterbury in 1633. In 1700 Thomas Cockshott, a farmworker from Tadcaster in North Yorkshire, perhaps fed up with having to answer doorstep enquiries, erected what was, in 1924, Britain's oldest surviving milestone. A good set of stones erected by the community marks the mile on each of the three main roads out of Aberystwyth in West Wales, though the majority of citizens could but dream of journeys to most of the places indicated.

Left: *A ticket from the toll bridge at Swinford, Oxford-shire, over which 1800 vehicles pass daily.*

Right: *A turnpike road boundary stone on the A10 near Ely, Cambridgeshire.*

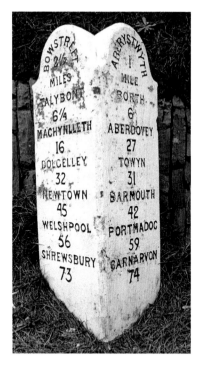

Left: *One of the three one-mile stones on roads out of Aberystwyth. This one is on the A487; the others are on the A44 and A4120.*

Right: *A Devon milestone using decimal distance (see page 28). Photograph courtesy of Tim Jenkinson.*

As travel grew so did complaints about the condition of the roads. The government became concerned and a number of Acts of Parliament established a system of gates across the roads, or turnpikes, to create revenue and manage the main network more effectively. The turnpikes were managed by trustees, who controlled access through the tollgates, usually at a tollhouse, and levied tolls. The money was used to build new roads and maintain existing ones. This extract is from a 1642 action before magistrates at Cirencester, before the law had changed to allow turnpike trusts to be set up:

> Each end of the High Street … was secured against a horse, with a strong straight boom which our men call Turn pike. A barrier with short metal spikes along the upper surface, placed across a road to stop passage till the toll has been paid.

The first turnpike trust was established in 1663 in Lincolnshire. Gates duly became the normal form of turnpike. The great majority were set up in the eighteenth century, serving major centres of industry,

A 1924 drawing of what was then the second oldest surviving milestone in Britain, the milestone erected by Thomas Cockshott of Tadcaster in 1700. The oldest was Oxford's 1667 one-mile marker stone – see page 40.

A milestone on the Bath Road at Purton in Wiltshire.

commerce, tourism and learning. So many people were visiting Bath to take the waters that turnpike roads radiated from the city like the spokes of a wheel.

The charges were not always popular and there were many protests and riots. As the turnpikes were government property the penalty for damaging them was anything up to deportation or execution. That epic of travel literature, *Coaching Days and Coaching Ways* by W. Outram Tristram, published in 1888, reports one such story from the Exeter road. At a tollgate near Ilchester a coach-driver was told to resist the demands of the toll-keeper, who was in arrears in his payments to the trustees. Refused access, he grudgingly paid but further obduracy at the next gate resulted in fisticuffs, with victory to the coach crew and the opening of the gate. William Cobbett, in his equally compelling *Rural Rides* of the 1820s, disliked turnpikes: 'Those that travel on turnpike roads know nothing of England', an observation that could equally apply to motorway travel today.

Both of these books generously cite distances travelled and this suggests an abundance of milestones. Turnpike trusts were encouraged from the early 1740s to mark every mile and in 1766 it became obligatory. Mile-markers allowed accurate pricing and timing of journeys, enabling stagecoach drivers to adhere to their schedules and timetables.

The important road-maker Thomas Telford designed not just roads but tollgates, tollhouses and bridges, as well as his own distinctive milestones. He worked on the Holyhead road, building a virtually new road through North Wales and setting new standards of construction. A few of Telford's stones

A drawing by Hugh Thomson of a fight at a tollgate.

12

A 'classical' milestone design by Thomas Telford for the road he built to Holyhead.

HOLY-
HEAD
106 - M
SALOP
O M-6F

Above right: *The Isle of Arran has all its stones in place.*

Left: *A Derbyshire mile-marker on the A6. The road surface has risen greatly since the post was erected.*

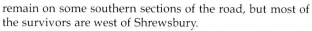

Below: *A distinctive Staffordshire type of marker at Bradnop on the A523/A52 Leek to Ashbourne road. All are in place. Rather similar types are found in Derbyshire and Cheshire.*

remain on some southern sections of the road, but most of the survivors are west of Shrewsbury.

On most British roads the evidence of milestones is patchy. Where there has been less disturbance, more milestones remain. Reasonable lengths of road with many of their original markers still do exist, including the complete set on the island of Arran. The A52/A523 (Ashbourne to Leek) and A620/B6079 (Retford to Worksop) roads have complete runs. The A6 in parts of Derbyshire, Lancashire and Cumbria has good, varied representation of types, while in Buckinghamshire the A413 from Buckingham to the A40 at Denham and the A40 thence to Stokenchurch are similarly well served.

Early milestones, whether set up by private individuals or turnpike trusts, were usually square or cylindrical, though a flat tombstone shape also occurred. Local stone rapidly replaced early wooden examples, with rare 6 foot English slate examples from Swithland in Leicestershire at 15 shillings a stone; one survives at Ashby. At first, faces were square to the road but, as travel became faster, angled designs emerged for better visibility. For similar reasons Roman numerals gave way to Arabic. Some stones were elaborately shaped, as on the A30 near Exeter and Basingstoke.

The arrival of cast-metal plates enabled old, worn and therefore insufficiently informative stones to be upgraded. Casting allowed for more detail, and resistance to erosion. Many stone examples were simply replaced as all-metal types emerged. Many of these took the angled form but incorporated a sloping or dished upper panel, which gave even more information, often the distance to London or the name

of the locality. Some Yorkshire turnpike trusts had the name of the road recorded in this space.

Turnpike trustees sometimes sought more feasible routes. The vicar of one worried community, which was to be bypassed if a proposed re-routing went ahead, wrote to the trustees, emphasising the community's dependence on passing trade and begging for a reprieve. Across the bare landscapes between Salisbury in Wiltshire and Blandford Forum in Dorset several different routes were tried and later disowned, surviving now as minor roads or tracks and green lanes.

Left: *One of several milestones found on the A413 between Buckingham and Aylesbury.*

Left and far left: *Two distinctive types on the original Carlisle (A6) road between Preston and Kendal.*

Above left and right: *Old and new types on the A496 Barmouth to Harlech road.*

Left: *Old and new types on the A513 at Elford, Staffordshire.*

Plain numbered examples from the old King's Lynn to Hunstanton road in Norfolk (at Ingoldisthorpe) (far left) and the old Aberdeen to Braemar route (near Corgarff) (near left).

15

Far left: *Letters and numbers only on a stone on the A683 in the former Westmorland (now Cumbria): KL = Kirkby Lonsdale; S = Sedbergh.*

Left: *Abundant detail on an old Ayrshire stone at a road junction on the A77.*

Below: *A milestone of Welsh slate on the A4085 near Betws Garmon, Gwynedd.*

Two elaborate designs, on the A379 near Exeter (left) and the A30 near Basingstoke (above).

Several fine stones with hands can be found on the A646 road from Halifax in West Yorkshire to Burnley in Lancashire. Variations in spelling occur in some older examples.

The milestone above, on the A640 at Outlane, West Yorkshire, shows the surveyor's name. The milestone (left) with cuffed hands is at Long Preston on the A65 in North Yorkshire. The modern distance between Skipton and Settle is 16 miles! The stone on the right, dated 1802 and also showing the names of the surveyors, is at Burley, Hampshire.

Left: *Guidance above a shop in Totton, near Southampton.*

Right: *A milepost on the A65 Kendal road, well repainted by the Yorkshire Dales National Park Authority.*

Left and below: *Flat metal-plate milestones from the A814 at Rhu near Helensburgh, in Argyll and Bute, and on the original A50 (now A511) north of Burton upon Trent, Staffordshire.*

Top left and centre left: *Two Leicestershire angled metal mileposts from the original A427 (now A4304), the one on the left with upper sloping panel featuring the royal arms.*

Top right and centre right: *Two angled metal mileposts, one from the A16 in Lincolnshire and one from the A511 (formerly the A50) in Staffordshire.*

Left and below: *Distinctive metal designs from the A638 (former A1) north of Bawtry, South Yorkshire, and the A40 at St Clears, Pembrokeshire.*

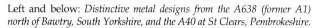

The first two stones on the drove road from Bishop's Castle to Craven Arms in Shropshire. The second (left) is on the old straight route continuing the first straight mile and reveals an older type; the modern road curves after the first stone and takes a different direction for several miles. This is a good example of an old stone on a 'lost' route.

Stone markers on deserted routes were simply left to deteriorate. Many went as building stone for local farmers. The inscriptions on one survivor along the old Roman road out of Heddington in Wiltshire, which had become part of the original coach route to Bath (although it is now just a track), have totally eroded, but the stone still forms part of the story of travel. A better-preserved example exists near Shaftesbury, close to the line of an old drove road across Salisbury Plain.

The old Derby Road ended with this intriguing statement on a stone in a wall at Uttoxeter, Staffordshire: 'Termination of the Derby Road Derby 18 miles one 1/4 & 50 yds'.

Where Ogilby found the Roman network echoed on his maps, so the turnpike trustees affirmed and extended it, shaping the patterns that survive today. Small eighteenth-century road atlases by Cary and Bowen, based on Ogilby, showed the expansion in travel the turnpike trusts had brought about. The turnpike system endured well into the nineteenth century, with upwards of 19,000 road miles (30,000 km) covered. One of the last turnpike trusts to be authorised was on the Kennett and Amesbury road in Wiltshire in 1840, and renewal Acts were passed regularly until as late as 1879.

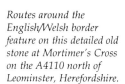

Routes around the English/Welsh border feature on this detailed old stone at Mortimer's Cross on the A4110 north of Leominster, Herefordshire.

19

Features of milestones and mile-markers

Wood was a natural early material. East Sussex records show that in 1672 the Flimwell and Hastings trust commissioned a series of wooden mileposts at 12 shillings each. As we have seen, cast-metal plates could be fastened to older, worn wood. In Brailes in Warwickshire two metal plates are fixed to wooden posts, as is the case with many of the Sussex Bow Bells series along the A22 (see opposite).

Nevertheless, stone was more durable, fairly abundant and, notwithstanding carving costs, relatively inexpensive. With the onset of industrialisation metal became increasingly available and in time a cheaper option. The basic design would be cast in metal and in some cases, for economy, a marker was customised, using a separate smaller metal plate affixed to give the information for that stone. Good examples survive in Norfolk on the B1105 out of Fakenham, while the A1067 mileposts show confusion in the casting and placement of individual examples in relation to the distance to Norwich. Mileposts out of Newcastle towards Morpeth on the old A1 had the Newcastle distance cast but the Morpeth information on separate plates. In Northumberland initials only were sometimes used, as on the Morpeth stones and those on the Rothbury ('RB') to Hexham ('H') road.

Above: *A milestone on the B1105 near Fakenham, Norfolk, with studs showing where pieces of plate are missing.*

Right: *An original A1 marker: the mileage from Newcastle (N) has been cast but the mileage from Morpeth (M) has been cast separately and attached.*

The decorative Sussex markers just mentioned are known as Bow Bells milestones because their distinctive design includes a bow and a string of bells. There has been some discussion as to the origin of the name. Bow in East London was a popular reference point but it is unlikely that a road south of the Thames would have been measured from it. Tristram affirms the route via East Grinstead and Lewes as 'fifty-eight miles two furlongs measured from the Surrey side of Westminster Bridge, which is the point from which the Brighton Road is measured'. A flat marker on a wall in Lewes confirms that this was how the distance was measured. The Cyclists' Tourist Club (CTC) *Gazette* of 1924 suggested that the design represented the husk of *Garrya elliptica* (a plant grown for its attractive catkins) with simple additional ornamentation. The motif was used by Adam and Chippendale in the late eighteenth century, the

period when the markers were most probably erected, but *Garrya elliptica* was unknown in Britain at the time. (It was discovered in 1826 in Canada by Nicholas Garry.) Route adjustment in 1820 to avoid a bad hill changed the distance by half a mile, necessitating a new 35-mile marker, which featured a honeysuckle motif.

Metal plates could also be fixed to walls. The East Riding unitary authority in Yorkshire has several examples of metal

Above left and near left: *Mile-markers on the walls of buildings: at Elmham House on the B1110 in Norfolk, and on a cottage at Fulbrook on the A361 near Burford in Oxfordshire.*

Far left: *A mounting block on the A1033 in Winestead near Patrington in East Yorkshire.*

Far left: *The original A40 stones were re-carved but not always put back in the same place. This example at Halfway House, Loudwater, Buckinghamshire, started as Roman XXXI but became Arabic 27 half way to Oxford.*

Left: *An old carved angled stone on the original A45 at Kentford on the Suffolk–Cambridgeshire border was turned and given a new metal form by way of upgrading.*

plates fixed to mounting blocks, including one very well maintained example near Beverley almost 4 feet (1.2 metres) high, and another that was found 2 feet (60 cm) underground and restored. Another example of such 'double utility', on the original Stroud to Cheltenham route in Gloucestershire, now a back road, has also been restored.

Early stones might be turned and re-carved, or plated, to augment detail and improve visibility from faster stagecoaches. Stones so treated did not always return to their original locations.

Unlike Roman stones, most examples from the seventeenth and eighteenth centuries tend to be cuboid, with the faces each representing a different direction, and all four faces used at busy crossroads. The majority of surviving examples are on roads out of

Far left: *These interesting plates at Hinstock on the Shropshire stretch of the Chester Road (A41) hide evidence of earlier incised information.*

Left: *On the same road, nearer Wolverhampton, missing plates at Standford show the earlier inscription.*

The 'White Lady' obelisk on the old Portsmouth Road at Esher in Surrey, with a close-up of some of the destinations.

London and usually give only the distance to London. In Esher in Surrey one surviving stone shows only this, but to both Cornhill and Westminster Bridge.

Also at Esher, on the original Portsmouth Road, is a milestone erected through private or other local initiative, as in Aberystwyth. This fine, cylindrical 'White Lady' obelisk indicated many places, near and far, and a 1767 date. The similarly ancient but even more substantial obelisk on the present A49 at Craven Arms in Shropshire also gave a great number of destinations, including Berwick and Edinburgh, though one cannot imagine many of the local inhabitants contemplating such journeys. Other obelisks survive, sometimes commemorative in character; that erected by Sir M. T. Gott marked the spot near his Chalfont St Peter home in

The Craven Arms obelisk on the A49 in Shropshire, with a close-up of some of the destinations.

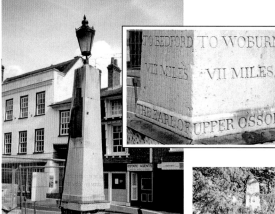

Left: *The obelisk at Ampthill in Bedfordshire, which doubles as a water pump, with a close-up of the lettering.*

Right: *The Belton obelisk in Lincolnshire on the original A607 doubled as a water trough (now used as a flower bed).*

Buckinghamshire where he realised he was not, after all, lost one evening. Beautifully sculpted hands adorn the St Ives obelisk in Cambridgeshire. In Bedfordshire, Ampthill's doubles as a water pump and, in Lincolnshire, Belton's as a water trough.

Not far from Craven Arms, at a crossroads near Clun, a local aristocrat erected a beautifully fretted metal guidepost to nearby villages, without distances. In Gloucestershire the renovated Teddington Hands obelisk on the Cheltenham to Evesham road marks six possible directions from that spot, but here distances are also given.

Sometimes arrows and hands pointed the direction, which otherwise had to be inferred from the angled faces. According to the CTC *Gazette* for 1923, the Ordnance Survey arrow on some stones (as on traditional convict clothing) indicated government property.

The finely sculpted hands of the obelisk on the A1123 at St Ives in Cambridgeshire.

The Teddington Hands obelisk at the junction of the A46, A435 and B4077 in Gloucestershire, not far from the obelisks at Beckford and Bredon just over the border in Worcestershire. The hands point in six directions.

Henry Sidney, Master of the Ordnance, allowed the use of the broad arrow that formed part of his crest.

Outside the Stanford estate in Northamptonshire large rectangular pillars on the approach roads give distances to local places as well as to the house itself, while a flat stone outside Felbrigg Hall in Norfolk does similar service.

While milestones provided continuous roadside guidance, directional stones and wooden or metal finger-posts, forerunners of modern signposts, served at road junctions. Well-documented examples in the Derbyshire and Yorkshire Pennines, known as 'guide stoops', often reflected older packhorse routes, pre-turnpike, and, where indicating distance, invariably used customary miles. These routes were favoured later as they were without tolls.

The Bredon (left) and Beckford (right) obelisks in Worcestershire, the latter restored in 1953 to mark the coronation of Queen Elizabeth II.

25

On either side of a quiet country lane, two massive pillars guide travellers to and from Stanford Hall in Stanford on Avon on the Northamptonshire–Leicestershire border. A third pillar is just in Leicestershire, near South Kilworth.

There was a great variety in the design of metal mileposts. The cylindrical types found in Derbyshire and Staffordshire influenced neighbouring Cheshire, where other distinctive designs, some reminiscent of the pages of a book, also occur. Mileposts in a similar, flatter style were used in Northumberland and Scotland, as were those in the form of a shield on an upright post, another distinctive local type. Some with angled sides and upper sloping face had a tapering shaft driven into the ground. The use of similar designs in different counties perhaps reflects standard manufacturing styles.

The unit of measurement could vary and fractions were a challenge. The road to Brighton via Reigate used eighths of a mile,

Above: *Classical styling for this type of marker near Wells in Somerset, a type also found in Dorset.*

Left: *At Felbrigg Hall, Norfolk, an ornate flat tombstone-type milestone guides travellers.*

A Cheshire example (top left) on the A537 of the 'circular stick' type of milepost found also in Staffordshire and Derbyshire, with two of Cheshire's more distinctive types near Knutsford (on the road to the M6) (top right) and Altrincham (on the A556; note the unusual spelling) (left).

Right: A distinctive shield type is found in Northumberland, but survivors are rarely undamaged, unlike this one at Horsley on the original A69.

Below: This type of milepost on the B6346 in Eglingham, Northumberland, is also found in Scotland.

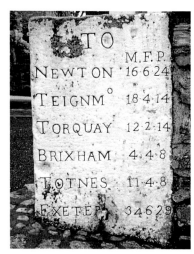

Variety existed in the way the distance was given. Here are four different examples: from Kingswear in Devon (miles, furlongs and poles) (top left); Haverstock Hill, London (miles and feet) (top right); the B3170 in Somerset (eighths of a mile) (below left); and Pembrokeshire (miles and yards) (below right).

as did a road in Somerset. Metal-on-stone markers in Pembrokeshire and a fine stone in Uttoxeter, Staffordshire, gave exact yards. Two London stones made reference to feet. Several Devon stones recorded miles, furlongs and poles. Cornwall and Norfolk used furlongs, as did Britain's oldest surviving dated milestone, from 1713, in Beckenham, Kent, and some very good ones near Otley in Yorkshire. Particularly confusing for travellers was the use on the same road, and even the same stone, of customary and statute miles or of Roman and Arabic numerals.

Fractions with Roman digits were ambiguous. 'II ¹/₂' could be read as eleven and a half instead of two and a half! The A1303 series in Cambridgeshire included 'VIIII' for nine. A few milestones in progressive series advised on arrival that there were 0 (zero) miles to go. Stones giving the distance to London as 100 miles are also appealing. In Warwickshire, that in Atherstone High Street had identical distances of 100 miles for Liverpool and Lincoln on its flanks but doubts about their accuracy led to their being replaced by the more humble, local, but still alliterative Lutterworth and Lichfield.

Between Tavistock and Bere Ferris, in part the B3257, are some old

There was variety in the presentation of digits. These four examples are from (clockwise from top left): a minor road near Fowey in Cornwall (Roman V); the A6 in Lancashire (Roman with Arabic fraction); the A1303 in Cambridgeshire (VIIII for 9); and A1071 at Hadleigh in Suffolk (Roman and Arabic).

granite stones with distances in old Devon miles, less than today's Statute miles. Among these one sees decimal distances as to Tavistock 4.9 and to Bere Ferris 1.1. The decimal point is most certainly not a blemish in the stone as the digits are sized differently (see page 11).

Occasionally one finds a stone with the single letter 'C' on it. This is believed to be a warning of a bridge or other river crossing within 100 yards.

Zero ('0') markers on the A917 at Kingsbarns, near St Andrews, Fife; the A413 at Winslow in Buckinghamshire; and the A338 at Fordingbridge in Hampshire.

Left: A 'C' stone at Ottery St Mary in Devon, indicating a bridge in 100 yards.

Above left: The 'London 100' stone in Atherstone High Street, Warwickshire, on the old line of the A5. It originally had 'Lincoln 100' and 'Liverpool 100' on its flanks but doubts were raised about the accuracy of these distances and more useful local indications were substituted.

Left: *One of several highly informative direction markers in the area around Cupar and St Andrews in Fife; some, as here at Higham Toll crossroads on the A915, show distances. There is another marker on the other corner of the junction that lists different information.*

Right: *Two mileposts that show the distance to the nearest railway station: on the B4451 at Deppers Bridge, near Harbury, Warwickshire; and on the Trent bridge road, the original A50 (now A511), at Burton upon Trent in Staffordshire.*

Above: *The A703 out of Peebles has a good, well-maintained series, giving the distance to the General Post Office at Edinburgh.*

Below: *This milepost (left) on the A821 in Stirling indicates The Trossachs Hotel, while an example on the A81 (right) indicates Aberfoil Inn and Glasgow's Royal Exchange.*

31

A small but attractive series on the A594 in Cumbria measures the distance to Cockermouth's court house; this marker has been incorporated into the adjacent farm wall.

Fife in Scotland, south of the Cupar to St Andrews road, has several large direction plates, some with distances, to many tiny local villages and even hamlets.

Occasionally, prominent buildings, railway stations, post offices, hotels and even inns have featured on distance markers.

Left: *One of several markers to be found around Bath, measuring to the Guildhall. This one is at the five-ways junction on the A365 near Box in Wiltshire.*

Below right: *On the A762 in Dumfries and Galloway there is a short series of milestones indicating the distance from New Galloway to New Galloway Station, 4 miles away. This is the third stone in the series. The railway station, marked only as 'N.G.St^n', no longer exists.*

Left: *Milestones along the A49 out of Ludlow in Shropshire use Roman numerals and measure to Ludlow, but this stone near Church Stretton cites Ludlow Cross.*

The modern era

In 1878 in Scotland and in 1888 in England and Wales highways became the responsibility of the new county councils, which became the legal owners of the milestones and markers. The councils also produced their own designs because many stones were illegible or had disappeared. Metal markers were more usual, often the angled type. Some designs were used by more than one county, perhaps with minor differences. Local foundries may have offered *á la carte*

Distinctive types found in particular counties (clockwise from top left): from the A372 in Somerset (also found in Dorset); the old A44 in Worcestershire; on the A1122 in Norfolk; and the A41 in Cheshire.

styles, which councils distinguished by use of their names or initials.

A rather wide and flat version marked the first mile from London on the old Great West Road, directly outside the Royal Geographical Society headquarters, near the Royal Albert Hall. Less than a mile away, outside the Milestone Hotel, is a later type by a different

Numbers XI and I of the Trinity Hall series in Cambridgeshire, the distinctive first stone (top right) and the more detailed stone at the junction with the present A505 (top left) affirming its earlier status as an important junction. The rest of the road is in Hertfordshire, where plates were fixed over the beautiful original inscriptions, as with Number XII (left).

Right: A large City of Westminster milepost (one mile to London) outside the Royal Geographical Society headquarters in Kensington, London. At 1¾ miles Kensington also put up a milepost.

council. Local streets, houses and hotels with 'milestone' in their name give valuable clues to the existence at some time of a stone, and some Ordnance Survey maps show milemarkers and can help unravel their fate.

The introduction of the motor car increased the speed and distance of travel. Early in the twentieth century the Automobile Association made enamelled circular plate distance markers and mounted them on the walls of

An AA plate on a wall in Bredon, Worcestershire.

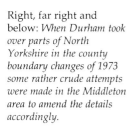

Right, far right and below: *When Durham took over parts of North Yorkshire in the county boundary changes of 1973 some rather crude attempts were made in the Middleton area to amend the details accordingly.*

buildings, often garages. Many have disappeared but some survive, in varying designs. There is an AA plate in Bredon in Worcestershire, high up on a brick wall.

The latter decades of the twentieth century have been a sad time for Britain's milestones. County councils, constrained by budget pressures and favouring modern signing over the older markers, have tended to neglect them. Many have been lost to road and other building construction, especially suburban shopping and

housing. Inscriptions have also worn away, while rain and frost have caused the stone to crack and flake. Rust and atmospheric contamination have reduced legibility and rendered mileposts brittle, vulnerable to collisions and the flails of modern verge-cutting

Far left: *The remains of a Northumberland shield milepost on the original A69 at Walbottle. Close by is an earlier stone marker.*

Left: *All that is left of a milestone inserted into the wall of the Saracen's Head hotel in Southwell, Nottinghamshire.*

machinery. Damaged or fallen stones are often ignored and ivy and nettles take over. Several have been rescued from building sites and council dumps. Part of the old 1851 Bridlington turnpike road collapsed into the sea – but no milestones were found on the beach! Even local government reorganisation can bring harm. Resulting scarcity and heritage interest now make theft a problem. A dealer trading in milestones is trading in stolen goods unless unambiguous proof of provenance is available.

At the start of the Second World War in 1939 the government presumed that any invading German army would lack maps, aerial surveys, compasses and even geographical skills and would thus be heavily dependent upon British milestones and signposts. To create

Above: *All that is left of an original sandstone marker on the B709 north-west out of Langholm, Dumfries and Galloway. It has probably been hit by verge-cutting flails or passing traffic.*

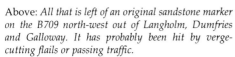

Right: *Number III in the Trinity Hall series was found by the author lying on its side in a lay-by near the M11 exit to Cambridge. The Highways Division of Cambridgeshire County Council was informed and the stone was repaired and re-sited further back.*

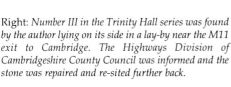

Above: *A milestone on the A4079 in Powys, just out of Hay-on-Wye and near the A479 junction. It has been left standing at an angle, painted and with surrounding vegetation killed off.*

Right: *One of the fine A49 series near Chorley in Lancashire, pictured in 1994 before it was stolen in 1998. Milestones remain public property, many of them listed, and any offered for sale may well be stolen unless solid proof of provenance is available.*

confusion, signposts were turned but milestones had to be buried or their detail erased. Stories are told of fathers or grandfathers digging ditches, toppling the stones in and covering them up. All should have been reinstated, in the towns in 1942 and elsewhere in 1943. Yet those along empty, open stretches of road may never have been restored. During excavations for the footings of two houses

At Nettlebed on the A4130 (formerly A423) Oxford to Henley-on-Thames road is a fine example of the original stones (far left). The next survivor (near left), two miles on, shows wartime defacement, as does that on the Fair Mile in Henley itself.

37

following the demolition of some cottages on the road to Epsom from Kingston in Surrey a milestone *was* found and duly re-erected by the local council. Metal mileposts may have disappeared into scrapyards and furnaces hungry for munitions fodder and been made into tanks, ships and gun-carriers but two buried markers have been found using metal detectors and an old Ordnance Survey map.

There used to be little interest in the heritage value of milestones but this is now changing. As there are so many reasons to explain the disappearance of milestones it is not surprising that in some counties they are scarce and in many others evidence is patchy. The Milestone Society exists to identify, record and conserve surviving examples through its county branches. English Heritage and Cadw in Wales now list mile-markers, while local authorities are gradually becoming sympathetic. Vigilance and a sense of responsibility are important. This could be helped by a simple code of conduct for verge-cutting, road improvement and building contracts that required any markers threatened by such projects to be identified and protected. Local businesses have already given money and materials to conservation groups. The use of heritage moneys and council staff for maintenance of markers or to provide materials for informed volunteers would be proper. Parish adoption schemes, as in Derbyshire, also help. One Derbyshire parish has appointed its own monuments warden. Heritage organisations, including the

Below left: An early stone at the Swindon end of the B4192 from Hungerford, widened to meet the A419 dual trunk road near the M4 junction. The stone is damaged but well painted.

Below right: A stone on the A85 near Lochearnhead in Stirling was commandeered as a gatepost with the house name and distance information combined.

Milestone Society, and professional conservation experts can provide guidance on conservation techniques. Publicising the heritage issues is vital.

There have been some well-meaning but misguided attempts at conservation. One Norfolk resident, keen to care for a county stone outside his house, painted it yellow. A milepost in the car park of a pub in Burton upon Trent in Staffordshire has had its text painted in the same red as the pub's exterior metalwork. And a resident of Lochearnhead in Stirling, Scotland, painted his very worn milestone but added his house name.

Study is also important. There are problems with reconciling the evidence from some markers. For example, two mileposts in Thirsk in North Yorkshire show different distances to London: were there two different routes, or is it a case of careless measurement? The more central one depicts what is assumed to be a drover but local opinion holds that it commemorates Tom the Tippler, a colourful local character. Further study into the origins, manufacturers, transportation and costs of milestones will reveal more of their story.

Milestones also remain in Tasmania, left over from the days of the British Empire. Canals had milestones and many remain, but that is a separate though similar story.

It was known that Chester and Oxford each had a set of markers, tall wooden posts and small stones respectively, marking one mile

Two mileposts at Thirsk, North Yorkshire, showing different distances to London. The one on the right depicts sheep on one face and a human figure on the other.

One of Oxford's remaining 'one-mile' stones, at the top of Morrell Avenue, marking the original Shotover route to Wheatley, where it joined Ogilby's Map 1 route into London from Aberystwyth.

from the city centre on the main exit routes (an Oxford stone, dated 1667, is the oldest extant British stone that refers to distance). To mark the start of the new millennium in 2000 some villages erected similar mile-markers on their exit roads.

To mark the new National Cycling Network new mileposts in black metal with gold lettering have been installed at key points along the routes. They give the cycling distances to the nearest towns, not necessarily the shortest routes.

Birmingham Airport has a splendid post outside its terminal building giving the distance by air in both miles and kilometres to several major foreign cities. Distances in kilometres may soon feature on signposts on British roads as Europeanisation gathers pace.

An unusual memorial stone at Newbold on Stour in Warwickshire on the old road from Oxford to Stratford-upon-Avon includes this verse, a fitting final testament to the interest intrinsic in the British milestone:

6 Miles
To Shakespeare's Town whose Name
Is known throughout the Earth
To Shipston 4 whose Lesser Fame
Boasts no such Poet's Birth

At Powfoot, on the Scottish shore of Solway Firth, this sign guides cyclists following the National Cycling Network.

Gazetteer

This list is not comprehensive but mentions the better examples, and represents the most recent evidence available to the author. Changes, especially to road numbering, may well occur, and new information is always welcome.

Bedfordshire
Very few remain, but the recent find of old 'plates' has seen several restored. There are some surveyors on 6 around Biggleswade, an example near Stotfold, & a private obelisk in Ampthill that doubles as a water pump.

Berkshire
Good early stones on A4 marked from Hyde Park Corner, scattered examples around Reading, Ascot, Bracknell, Wokingham and Maidenhead to Henley. Many lost to Oxfordshire in 1973.

Buckinghamshire
The A413 Denham (A40 junction) to Towcester road has good, almost complete sequences, especially Amersham to Buckingham. There is a private obelisk at Chalfont St Peter and a Reading to Hatfield turnpike trust obelisk at Marlow. A40 from Uxbridge to Stokenchurch has good sequences, and some evidence of re-use.

Cambridgeshire and Peterborough
Trinity Hall milestones along the original A10 and B1368; a long Roman-numeral series on A1303. There is a fine decorative obelisk at St Ives, and an interesting pillar on B1043 5 miles south of Huntingdon gives three routes to London. Milestones at Wansford on old A1 and London road in Peterborough. Scattered examples on A428, A603, A1198 (old A14) and A604. Some milestones on the old A604 survive despite dualling (now A14). The area around Thrapston and Kimbolton is worth exploring. There is a good series from the old turnpike (stones marked to London) on A45 and B660. An obelisk on the old A1 at Alconbury offers mileage to London for three routes.

Cheshire
Interesting range of designs including dated county types. The A437, B5470 and A56 are worth exploring, as are A57, A537 and A49 (especially around Tarporley) and B5152 to Frodsham. The Macclesfield and Holmes Chapel areas have some interesting examples.

Cornwall
Fine early examples on A30 near Redruth and to Land's End, especially Crows an Wra and local roads around St. Just. Road into Truro show good variety, including some just 'From Truro'. Some military stones just have numbers. Some places are signified by town initials, with 'L' needed local knowledge!

Cumbria
Good variety of types: rare Westmoreland example, and old mixed Roman/Arabic distance stone at Shap Inn among good run along A6; very good runs on A595/A596 Cockermouth to Carlisle roads (original A596 via Allonby) and A683/A65 out of Kirby Lonsdale; metal and stone types, including flat types, on A591 and near Elterwater and Cartmel; isolated stones near Alston; Nateby AA plate; rare distance and direction advice plate in house wall near Brough.

Derbyshire
There are 169 listed, including fifty in the Peak District national park. Some circular types along A6 with more variety north of Matlock. There are two styles on A61 at Clay

Cross and an interesting group of pre-turnpike moorland guide stoops above Holymoorside. The B5017, B5324 and B5035 are worth visiting, as are A52, A515, A38(T), and B5023 and A625 and the old track parallel to A57 north-north-east of Cutthroat Bridge and another track from Edensor to Chatsworth.

Devon
Evidence of use of miles, furlongs and poles, especially at Shaldon Bridge and the Dart slipway at Kingswear. Old 'miles' on stones near Bere Alstons including unique, rare use of decimal distances, old and new types (detailed plates) in Babbacombe, detailed plates elsewhere, a coloured example at Colyford and obelisk at Rousdon (both A3052). Survivors at A30/A35, A377/A379 and scattered early examples on mnor road south of Barnstaple. 'B' roads around Bideford are interesting, and there is an attractive stone in Musbury. Recently restored examples can be seen on the A38, an AA plate at Wigginton and 'C' stones at Ottery St. Mary, Topsham and on minor road off A380 near Gappah.

Dorset
A very good county, especially on A30, A35 and A354. There is a group of four on B3069 near Swanage. Areas around Poole and Weymouth are good as are the Bridport and Maiden Newton areas. Poole to Salisbury route over Martin Drive leaves a milestone 'lost' on what is now a "green lane" north of Craborne. There are distinctive 'classical' capped stones, for example on A30 2 miles west of Sherborne, and which can also be found in Somerset. Dorset seems to have shared two types with Somerset.

Durham
Examples at Easington and on A689 Stanhope to Alston road. Bowes parish has five well-maintained examples, four on A66. The A688 Bowes to Durham road has almost a complete sequence.

Essex
The east and south-east areas are worth exploring, around Rayleigh, Wickford and Rochford, and also around Brentwood, Ingatestone and Hatfield Peverel (original A12) and the border with Hertfordshire. Some on Epping Forest roads. The B1383 and B1393 are good; the A414 and B181 have some examples. Patchy elsewhere but scattered across the county, though many are worn.

Gloucestershire, including Bristol
There has been well-endowed and significant restoration/conservation interest here. The A38 in and out of Bristol and areas around Stroud, Cirencester and Tetbury are good. Milestone at Minchinhampton says 100 miles to London.

Hampshire
A well-endowed county, with widespread representation. The A30 and original A34 are good to explore with connecting minor roads. Romsey and Ringwood have variety, including rare surveyors' names on a stone at Burley and a '0' marker in Fordingbridge. The areas around Andover and Portsmouth are worth exploring. An unusual example above a shop at Batts Corner, Totton.

Herefordshire
There were turnpikes in the 1730s on the main roads into Wales and the Borders with lesser A roads worth exploring. The A44, A49, B4361, B4224 and the area near Old Forge have some coverage. Generally scattered coverage, however, but many more known as recently as the 1980s. A40 example at Lea.

Hertfordshire
The old Cambridge to London route through Barkway has the later Trinity Hall series with county plates. The A10 has a good run. Parts of the old St Albans to Reading turnpike

trust route are well covered. B roads and minor A roads are better (A1198, A1170, B1368, B197). Scattered examples elsewhere. The Potters Bar to Hatfield road has early stones with evidence of plates that have been removed.

Kent
Maidstone and Tunbridge Wells, and the east coast and Sussex borders, have scattered examples including minor road with stones using only Roman numerals. Two are by pubs in Dartford and Hythe; there is another example near Bexley High Street. A plated stone at Hawkhurst on A268.

Lancashire
A good county to explore. The A6 has good variety. The A59 and A49, and main roads into Yorkshire industrial centres, are worth searching, especially the Saddleworth area and A646 east of Burnley. The areas around Blackpool, Preston and Kirkham have examples, as do Burnley and Clitheroe. There are distinctive types on A49 near Chorley.

Leicestershire
There are some well-maintained metal examples, some with the royal coat of arms, in the Lutterworth area. The A47 Leicester to Uppingham road has several stone survivors. There are rare slate examples at Ashby and Quorn and a fine unusual metal type on the old main road to Burton near Bosworth. There is an attractive stone at Burbage. The Stanford Hall pillar is near South Kilworth. The B577 old London road from Hinckley, A607 east of Melton, and the Rempstone to Ashby turnpike road are worth exploring. There is a Roman milestone in the Jewry Wall Museum in Leicester.

Lincolnshire
There are some milestones on A15, A16, A17 and A52. The Bourne, Holbeach and Boston areas are worth exploring. At Belton there is a water-trough obelisk on A607 and another obelisk is at Normanton.

London and Middlesex
Kensington is mentioned in the text and Haverstock Hill (post office at 45 feet example), Finchley and Golders Green. Examples also at Pinner, near the Swan pub at Stanwell, in the Torrington Park area, on A4 near Heathrow and Colnbrook, on A30 near Ashford Hospital, on A5 Holyhead road at Cricklewood, on A308 near Hampton Court, at Herne Hill and on Clapham Common. Local surveys show even more, especially North London.

Norfolk
A well-endowed county, with about 350 surviving milestones. The ones on the B1440 old road from King's Lynn to Hunstanton use numerals only. There is an obelisk at Holt. Example on the wall of Elmham House on B1110. Also Felbrigg Hall example. Dereham, Castle Acre and Swaffham areas have survivors. Examples on A149 and in the Fakenham area, especially B1105 and A1067. There is also a rare Yarmouth example of distance carved into pavement edge to guide seaside walkers.

Northamptonshire
Survivors very patchy here: long stretches of road with little or no evidence. There are notable pillars on the approaches to Stanford Hall, Stanford on Avon. The Thrapston area is better. There are two plateless Telford stones on A5 south of Weedon and another in Daventry (new plate). A few plateless survivors on the Towcester to Weston turnpike road (mostly A43). Plate with '0' in wall in Towcester High Street (A5).

Northumberland
There is a Roman stone at Vindolanda on Hadrian's Wall off A69 and a fine shield-type on the same road at Horsley. Several types on B6342 Rothbury to Hexham road. The B6346

at Eglingham has an unusual metal marker. Examples also on the original A1 Newcastle to Morpeth road, A68(T), A696 and A696(T), and on B roads near Corbridge. There are Roman milestones in the museum at Chesters Roman Fort.

Nottinghamshire
The 'Jockey' stone is at Jockey House junction at Elkesley on A1 and there is a milestone in Blyth on the original A1. There is a good run on A620 and B6079 between Retford and Worksop, notably at Babworth and Ranby. The A634 has several. There is an old, very worn stone in the wall of the Saracen's Head at Southwell. There are two tall pedestal types in Edwinstowe and Markham Moor, and an unusual style on A617 at Hockerton.

Oxfordshire
One-mile marker stones exist on early routes out of Oxford. Generally patchy but examples on B4044 to Swinford toll bridge, A423 Dorchester to Henley road (including texts erased in the war), on A329 south of Wallingford and on other former Berkshire roads, on A420, on the original A43 (see Northamptonshire), on A44 (originally A34).

Rutland
On A6121 at Ketton is a wartime survivor due to the initiative of a local farmer who buried and re-erected it. There are stone and metal types at the same place on the old A1 at Great Casterton. Examples on A6003 a mile south of Uppingham and a mile south of Oakham.

Shropshire
The county is well endowed with a good variety of milestones and mileposts, including Telford examples west of Shrewsbury. The Telford stone in Shrewsbury is one of four very different styles found in that town. The Shrewsbury–Shifnal road has a good run to Wellington reflecting an earlier Holyhead Road routing. Bishop's Castle to Craven Arms is good, with evidence of an older route 2 miles from Bishop's Castle. This area, including Clun, is worth exploring.

Somerset
The B3170 (off A303) to Taunton has a good series using eighths of a mile. A named county type near Clevedon. There are different distinctive county plates, especially on B3130 near Tickenham. Some designs were also used in Dorset. There are tablets in a wall

Apart from its Telford example, Shrewsbury has three other distinctive distance markers on roads out of the town. The garden-wall stone tablet is on the Hereford Road; it marks one mile to the town gates and may be similar to Oxford and Chester mile-markers. The other two are close to County Hall in the Shifnal direction.

at Yarlington (stone) off A303 and West Coker (metal) on A30. Bath Road Guildhall types occur west of Keynsham. The A30 has several. The B3170, A37 and A39 are worth exploring, as are the B3110 at Midford (for capped stones) and the area around Ilminster.

Staffordshire
Considerable residual stock here, mostly plain standard angled type, but designs more interesting on A50 (now A511) plus circular types on A515 and plated stones near Cheadle. Uttoxeter has 'TERMINATION OF THE DERBY ROAD DERBY 18 MILES ONE 1/4 & 50 Yds'. There is a tablet in a wall on A511 (former A50) plus an individual tablet in Tamworth with several destinations. Stone and metal are found at the same place on A513 at Elford.

Suffolk
Milestones are quite numerous according to the county council. Fine example at Woodbridge. Others in the area around Beccles, Bungay and Saxmundham, especially on A12 and A144 at Sudbury and on A134. Also in the Aldeburgh area and on A143 and B1113. Interesting obelisk at Hadleigh.

Surrey
There is the 'White Lady' obelisk at Esher and other examples in the Esher area generally. There are early types on A3 and on A22 near Reigate. Examples on A23 and A217 in the Horley area, on B2130, in Farnham centre and surroundings, two in Surbiton, at Wandsworth (listed) and on A30 at Egham. Good general representation.

Sussex
Long run of metal on wood 'Bow Bells' milestones (A22/A26) with Lewes shop wall plate giving two distances to Brighthelmstone from London; old stones on old Ashburnham private coach road near Battle; good general representation on A272/A283/A285/A24/A25/A26/A268/B2026; scattered examples elsewhere.

Warwickshire
Distinctive lamp-post style example in Shipston (old A34) now augmented by new 'finds' and local restoration. Shakespeare poem stoe at Newbold-on-Stour (also A34); a pair of metal on wood at Brailes and Rowington; four different types on A422 south from Stratford, and isolated examples on other roads but generally patchy. 'London 100' in Atherstone and Obelisk in Dunchurch.

Wiltshire
There is an old stone near Stonehenge on A303. The A30 and A4 are well covered. The Devizes area has 'boat' shape types. On the Bath Road are Guildhall types (e.g. Box area). Rare curved junction type at Box. At Purton a stone and tollhouse. Near Corsham a '100 to London' stone. Examples at Marlborough on A4 and private example near Cadley on A346 in Savernake Forest. Also on A420, and on roads into Salisbury and Warminster.

Worcestershire
County Council concrete types, especially near Alcester, Kidderminster and Bromsgrove; interesting older types on minor roads east of M5; examples on A44, 1449, B4204 and in Malvern, Evesham and Broadway areas (Take Off stone in Broadway); obelisks at Beckford and Bredon.

Yorkshire
Notable mounting-block types on roads into Beverley; early stones with decorative cuffs at Long Preston (A65), Outlane (A640 – rare example with surveyor's name) and Adel (1764). There are fine detailed examples on A660 stones near Bramhope; guide stoops, with some distances, on moors near Bradfield; double-sided 'old miles' junction stone near Sedbergh; interesting example on original A1 Blyth to Doncaster and York to

Thirsk/Northallerton; 'lost' packhorse route milestone on open moorland near A628; scattered examples on North York Moors and coast roads; decorative cast-irons in some cases (e.g. Ripon, Leyburn, Thirsk) but the majority are standard County Council types usually with named road (n.b. 1973 border changes significant).

Ireland (including Northern Ireland)
Highway management was originally under British auspices and milestones reflect this. Outside the north, mileages have changed to kilometres and this has affected their survival. Occasionally, political tensions have also made their mark (e.g. 'Dublin' has been blacked out on a stone just in the UK, near Pettigo). There is a generally a scattered representation across Ireland, and a good selection near coasts above and below Belfast.

Scotland
Fife is rich in old, interesting cast designs. On A90 at Inchture (old A85) a fine example with just initials and numbers. A long, plain-numbered series out of Aberdeen on B9119 and A944 to Braemar. Standard column types on roads into and around Stirling and Trossachs, also Tarbert to Campbeltown. Good areas around Dunoon, roads north of Glasgow, and in Ayrshire, especially around A77 and roads into Girvan. A fine individual design on A703 and A701 from Peebles to Penicuik and Edinburgh. Scattered examples on A9 north of Inverness to Wick. Arran, Jura, Mull and other islands with good sets. Examples on A884 and A861 between ferries at Lochaline and Corran. Also on A75 at Dumfries and A86 near Kingussie. Plate with many place-names in Dumfries town hall.

Wales
Unique, rare 1768 example 4 miles from Lampeter naming sight men (affirming early line of sight system for measurement). The A5 has Telford stones after Oswestry and on to Holyhead, and distinctive types lie around Haverford West/Tenby, also from M4 to Bridgend, and three one-mile marker stones on roads leaving Aberyswyth. The A44 in and out of Rhayader is well-served, new and old types can be seen together on A496 near Harlech and Builth Wells, a very good run from Cardigan to Lampeter, and scattered examples on A40, A4070, A4059, B4394, in Cardiff centre and roads around Machynlleth. Slate examples on Lleyn peninsula and across Gwynnedd, with small fractions in distances.

This plate in the wall of Dumfries Town Hall records several locally useful distances, but how relevant was Huntingdon?

Below right: A straightforward Dorset milestone hidden in undergrowth near Charmouth on the A35. The government arrow shows up well.

Restored to independent administration, Rutland will be proud of its surviving stones like this near Uppingham on the A6003.

46

Further reading

Cobbett, William. *Rural Rides*. London, 1853.
Cox, Benjamin G. *The Vale of Evesham Turnpikes, Tollgates and Milestones*. Vale of Evesham Historical Society, 1980.
Famous Milestones. National Benzole publication.
Haines, Carol. *Marking the Miles*. Self-published, 2000. (Available from the Milestone Society.)
Haynes, R.I.E. 'Buckinghamshire Milestones', in *Bucks Life*, November 1966.
Haynes, R.I.E. 'Wiltshire Milestones', in *County Councils Gazette*, 1968.
Hindle, Brian Paul. *Roads and Trackways of the Lake District*. Cicerone Press, 1998.
Hurley, Heather. *The Old Roads of South Herefordshire*. Pound House, 1992.
Lee, Joyce, and Dean, Jon. 'Where to? How Far?', in *Leicestershire Historian*, 2000.
Martineau, Hugh D. 'Milestones in Lincolnshire', in *Lincolnshire Life*, December 1973.
Rosevear, Alan. *Turnpike Roads to Banbury*. No. 10 in a self-published series about roads across the Thames Valley.
Rosevear, Alan. *Milestones and Toll-houses on Old Turnpike Roads*. No. 14 in the same series.
Sedgley, Jeffrey P. 'The Roman Milestones of Britain'. British Archaeological Reports, No. 18, 1975.
Smith, Howard. *Guide Stoops of Derbyshire*. Self-published, 2000.
Smith, Howard. *The Guide Stoops of the Dark Peak*. Self-published, 1999.
Thompson, Ruth and Alan. *The Milestones of Arran*. Self-published, 1999.
Tristram, W. Outram. *Coaching Days and Coaching Ways*. Macmillan, 1888.

Cyclists' Touring Club *Gazettes* and turnpike trust records in county record offices and museums are also worth consulting.

The Milestone Society (Secretary: John Atkinson) may be contacted at Hollywell House, Hollywell Lane, Clows Top, Kidderminster DY14 9NR.

A unique curved stone distance marker at the junction of the A4 and the A365 at Box in Wiltshire. It shows Marlborough in both directions.

Index of places